Scarlet Tiger

By the same Author

The Cansos *and* Sirventes *of the Troubadour Giraut de Borneil: A Critical Edition* (1989)

TWO + TWO (1997)

Birth of the Owl Butterflies (1997)

Scarlet Tiger

For Val
warmest wishes
& so lovely to meet you
Ruth 23/06/19

Ruth Sharman

Templar Poetry

Published in 2016 by Templar Poetry

Fenelon House
Kingsbridge Terrace
58 Dale Road, Matlock, Derbyshire
DE4 3NB

www.templarpoetry.co.uk

ISBN 978-1-911132-10-3

A CIP catalogue record of this book is available from the British Library

Cover Design and Artwork by Templar Design

Typeset by Pliny

Printed in England

Acknowledgements

My thanks to the editors of the following magazines, where some of these poems first appeared: *Poetry London*, *The Interpreter's House*, *Angle*, *Prop*, *Dream Catcher*, *Interlitq, English Writers 3* and *The Moth*; also to the editors of the following anthologies: *The Ring of Words: Poems from The Daily Telegraph Arvon International Poetry Competition 1998; Parents* (Enitharmon) and *A Twist of Malice* (Grey Hen Press). The title poem of this collection was a runner-up in the Troubadour International Poetry Prize 2007 and was published on the Troubadour website.

Special thanks also to Radio 4 – and in particular Melissa Viney – for broadcasting an interview relating to "The Song Inside" in *Something Understood* (January 2015), and to Jesse D. Lawrence for his short film *Borderlands*, part of a sequence devoted to the theme of special places and the relationship between place, inspiration and art.

The list of those who have offered me editorial support and/or encouragement over the years is long. Warmest thanks to Nadine Brummer, Beatrice Garland, Emily Maguire, Stephen Payne, Graham Townsley, Sara Lee Roberts, Phillip Nicholl and Ian Pople, and also to Francis Deas, Rosie Jackson, Rachael Clyne, Dawn Gorman, Stephen Boyce, Sue Boyle, Morag Kiziewicz and Chaucer Cameron.

for my father and my son

CONTENTS

III

I

By heart

Because we're running out of time
for you to talk and me to listen,
I want to get things straight –

to know which brood of holly blue
feeds on ivy, spring or summer,
and what distinguishes the gatekeeper

from the meadow brown, at twenty feet.
To hear you talk of flight patterns
and favourite plants, how wood whites drift

like snowflakes in the sun,
and even where the devil's bit persists,
the marsh fritillary's now rare.

I want you to remind me what was special
about that hairstreak with the W
scrawled in white across its underwing –

as if knowing cancelled absence
and a father could be hoarded
piecemeal with the facts –

and, just in case, I'm keeping count
of all the times we've watched
and waited and given names to things,

remembering what you say
about natural things growing subtler
the more they're magnified,

while the opposite seems true for us;
and how we tried to stir up clouds of wings
by hurling branches at a summer oak

but only caught a glimpse of silver –
though we knew for sure a whole colony
was feeding there, high up on the honeydew.

Leaving

That was December too when we cleared
our mother's dressing-table drawers
and found those prayer books, the hoard
of newspaper cuttings about cancer cures
and all her lipsticks with silly, flirty names
like Super Nectar and Love that Pink, now as dry
as the old trunk road before the monsoons came.
No earthly use. And heaven knows why
there were so many the same, so many cashmeres
still wrapped in cellophane, good as new,
reminding us of her unlived years...
And now you're anxious to know who
will give house room to the paddy birds
whose broken beaks are pointing at the sky,
to the cabinet your grandfather carved
from rosewood, and the photographs that lie
stranded in boxes muddling views
of "Travancore with prickly pear"
and cousins in ruched swimsuits
squinting on the beach at Scarborough.
Since even they have to go for want of space,
along with china, rugs and silverware,
that pouffe with the swallowtail in pride of place –
things we took for granted, knew were there
but barely noticed till now – on this winter's day
as a last ribbon of brightness stretches like a thinning artery
along the sky, and it all seems light years away.
Our childhood. Your India.

My father's note

It's been happening by degrees,
the way they said it would:

mowing the lawn takes two goes
with a stop for tea

and though none of us admits it
you're grassing over the beds

to save on labour, and then you're falling
in the field behind the house,

the air rasping in and out of your lungs
like nails on emery board,

barely tottering fifty yards
to the football pitch to see your grandson

named man of the match,
your legs like driftwood, angled

so awkwardly it's a wonder
they support your weight;

and by the time you need that chair
to get down the stairs

it's over with the woods
and the wild places

and all your butterflies are second hand,
copied from books in blurry watercolours.

But the way I see you
you're still darting

down some forest track,
pursuing a flash of blue or silver,

flipping your net over
with a practised flick of your wrist

and easing the contents
into your killing jar.

Or leaning, pin poised,
not daring to breathe

as you fix a soft abdomen in place –
with the same fingers

that scrawl this note to me now,
nineteen everyday words flitting about

as if they were searching
for nectar in a patch of sun.

Creedy Ward

Asleep, you look like Rameses
three thousand years
into the afterlife,
but I can still bring you back,
briefly, to snowdrops
and reports of scarlet tigers
so abundant they've been coming up
through the floorboards
and have to be rescued from the cats.
You're making sense
of commonplaces: you are
skin and bone, you are
what it means to *waste away*,
and as I snip your eyebrows
and shave the thin white stubble
from your neck and chin
I think of last year's tigers
in the kitchen, their bright bodies
lengthening and fattening
on brambles and anchusa,
then lying motionless one morning
among leaves and debris,
all the light gone out of them.
Blurred copies of themselves. And how
we rifled through potato peelings
and cellophane wrappers
to retrieve them from the bin
when you told us they weren't dead,
simply on the point of pupating.

The enemy

You jumped at Arnhem
and got a bullet in the groin,
another lodged behind your skull.
Dulled the pain with a shot
of brandy and a fag, and carried on.
But now your body's caving in
and everything hurts, even
clipping your toenails or levering
at your lips with a teaspoon.
You're too feeble to hotch
your bottom up the bed
but still insist you'll be better
by your birthday... *I can't see*
the enemy! You say it
out of the blue, staring wildly
round the room, as if you hoped
to catch Death skulking
in a corner or squatting
behind the dialysis machines,
and when a doctor marches
past your bed, for a second
you fix him with your sights,
then mow the bugger down.

Moth

You'd have known at a glance
what this one was.

I wanted to memorise it, hoping
you'd say it was special,

a rare migrant, perhaps, or a denizen
of marshes or riverbanks

attracted to our garden
against the odds,

like that scarlet tiger
your grandson found on the lawn.

It would have been a gift,
but seconds after I saw it

I'd forgotten where
its spots were and whether

those forewings were more purple
or bronze. And nothing

in the book seems to match.
Not the golden Y.

Not the common vapourer
or the marbled carpet…

No name then. Just a brief vision
of grace advertising itself

to a mate and warning off
the birds with its brightness.

Fragments

So, where does time go?
All the days of our lives,
the hours we've spent waiting
for buses, or rehearsing
conversations round and round
in our heads? Isn't it there still,
located in brain cells,
each moment freighted
with every moment gone
before, the memory of people,
places, things? Fragments
reach us now and then
from those distant galaxies –
tiny, random and bright,
like that moment in the garden
when we stood watching
a trail of mercury in sunlight,
so far away we couldn't be sure
if they were geese or swans.

Morphine

You look so far away when you're sleeping
they might have embalmed you for the afterlife
with bandages and balsam, nothing
but skin and bone, so slight I could almost lift you over
the side of the bed, your limbs bird-light,
skin, like a fritillary, chequered with shadows,

your mouth a cave of shadows,
and you dream you're fighting wars again, so even sleeping
brings no relief, wake as if we'd shone a flashlight
in your eyes and you were running for your life.
The drugs are tiding you over,
but your heart, kidneys, lungs, nothing

works as it should and there's nothing
to do but sleep and dream. A shadow's
showing on your liver, and your arm is black all over
since you bent your elbow, sleeping,
and blew your fistula… How much more of this half-life
can you bear, this second-hand light,

recycled air? You can't tell dark from daylight.
Even your lips, even your toenails hurt, and nothing
is easy – eating, breathing – your life
dependent on needles and tubes, the shadows
of your blood pulsing under plastic while you're sleeping,
your heart just ticking over.

Knowing it will soon be over
they've turned your bed away from the light
so they can watch you from the doorway while you're sleeping.
That's the last, then, of the trees and sky – nothing
to see but passing shadows
and that calendar counting down the days of your life

on a whitewashed wall. And it's not life
I wish for you now. It's for this to be over.
For you to dream you're back among the shadows
watching your evening browns flying in the last light
on India's southern tip. Then nothing,
no enemy, no butterflies, as you slip away, still sleeping.

At the LHC lecture

Imagine abbreviating a butterfly –
the silver washed fritillary for instance
commonly known as the SWF…
I was hoping for greater clarity,
but these hadrons and muons and gluons
are too minute to grasp,
and even supposing Big Bang
where will we find the last Russian doll?
If matter accounts for only four
per cent of all there is, then where
and what are you? Are you energy now?
Are you light or dark? Dispersed
or reabsorbed? Or like one of those
birthday candles you can't blow out?
All I can picture is a frantic darkness
with not a single point of rest
and you forever hurtling away from me
at almost the speed of light.

Silver washed fritillaries

You were right: it was never
just about butterflies – your fritillaries,
for instance, that were less washed
with silver than this landscape. Yes,
it was about you, my shy, awkward,
complex father, a way of connecting.
And it's about being your eyes now
and reporting back (as if such a thing
were possible), making a mental note
of the first white violets piercing
winter debris, or this sea of grasses
flowing towards a hill that's been singled out
for special attention by the light,
and how the silver wash takes us
circling back to those afternoons
watching for your butterfly in Neroche.
You told me just before you died
you thought *something* carried on,
though you wouldn't commit yourself
to words like God or Heaven,
and after all these were your church
and your religion, the woods and fields,
all the intricacies of butterflies and plants
you trusted as evidence of purpose
and design. But isn't this the only way
you live on, in these flimsy connections
between butterflies and light, between sky
and grasses and a name? Then why
does it feel wrong to have poured you
into the hard ground rather than let you fly
free of earth, weight and limitations,
scattering your atoms over the wide hills

or in some opening in the woods
where fritillaries settle on bramble flowers,
lifting wings not feebly washed
but jagged with bolts of silver lightning?

Quirks

All that's left is a collection
of butterfly books, a few watercolours
you painted in your latter years,
and memories of you charging
round the garden with the mower,
or furiously attacking a flower bed
with your fork. You disdainful
of dark glasses and foreign food,
genuinely wondering why people
did the things they do. Obsessing
over stair carpets and the spines
of books, loving wilderness but clinging
to a sense of order, always anxious
to name, identify, record and count –
how many slices you could cut
from a single banana, how many holes
you'd made in the lawn to let in air.
The only person I ever knew
who liked being hungry, cold or tired,
who said being stung by nettles
left him feeling more alive.
Who told me marbled whites
lay their eggs at random in the grass.
That I should run downhill from
an elephant and uphill from a bear.
And – one thing drummed into you
by your Victorian teacher-parents –
always to beware of strong emotion.

Brown hairstreak eggs

It's become a habit now, to stop
at every blackthorn bush and scrutinise
its branches, examining the base
of each spine and bud. "Conspicuous",
the book says, but *she* didn't mean them
to be seen and lays them at random,
maybe two to a bush, indistinguishable
from all the other pale anomalies
in the blackthorn's bark: pinpricks
of white that turn softly green in the path
of lichen and seen under glass are whorled
like the tops of those cottage loaves
they used to serve in the Lyons Café.
I never find them now. Is time running out
for *Thecla betulae*, described in the book
as "Range declining"? Or were we
just lucky, our two pairs of eyes better
than one as I searched the garden hedge
while you steadied the ladder?

Talking to myself

Just as a fly buzzing in the stillness
and a ladder of sunlight falling
across the floor of a shuttered room
carry the full DNA of summer,
it's only obliquely, almost by stealth,
that I can recall your face,
like an after-image where features,
a particular look, are subsumed
in a split-second's illumination,
and the inconsequential memories
are like the sound of that fly
in the shadowy room – charged
with the energy of a father
I can still picture counting fork holes
as he prods the lawn to let in air
or running at the double to fetch
the cap he left in a field five miles back,
who felt most at home in bogs
and on tangled hillsides watching
for the likes of this butterfly
that's just come flittering over
the garden fence and offers me
an excuse to keep talking – as if
you were still part of the four per cent
that is matter, a hand capable
of writing a note, a voice
still speaking on the end of a phone.

The June Gap

Everywhere you looked
you saw signs of change,
of habitats shrinking,
resident species on the point
of dying out, and yet
you named more butterflies
than I can call to mind –
flying despite the loss
of hedgerows, hay meadows
and grasslands, despite
the climate or the time of year,
passing like leaf shadows
over the tiny suns of cinquefoil.
Grizzled skipper,
marsh fritillary, duke
of Burgundy, painted lady,
marbled white... Years
have passed since then,
but what stays with me
is how focused you were
on what was missing,
what we *might* have seen;
and how hard I tried
to put names to colours,
patterns and styles of flight
but only ever caught
a mottled blur, a sense
of smaller or larger wings,
before the whatsitsname
was already flying
in a clearing further on.

Dancing

So what we'll do is slide the catch,
then lean in close and breathe…

As carefully as you pushed them home,
we'll pull out every heart-pin

and use our fingertips to smooth
each ruffled scale and shattered wing.

We'll watch the colours slowly deepen
to the shades they used to be –

the sharpening up of citrus, brilliance
restored to bands of blood-red eyes.

We'll see blue lightning leap
from jungle shadows,

black rivers zigzag
across the fragile ground of pure white maps,

and as the boxes fill with air
we'll see the first ripples disarrange

                    your ordered rows
and the strongest flyers lifting –

soaring birdwings and easy sailers,
the tawny rajah and the blue nawab,

then tortoiseshells and skippers,
tree nymphs, satyrs, lacewings –

the first few floating free,
then all the others darting, circling,

crowding upwards in the warmth,
too many names to name or colours to distinguish,

all their neat italic labels
muddled by the wind, not mattering

when this one flew at Periambadi,
or this at Travancore,

as we watch them flying in the last light
and can't see the sky for dancing.

II

Phugtal

Imagine waking to so much sky,
the river reduced

to a thread of light.
Couldn't wind just knock

this monastery off the mountain,
send it tumbling

like a wasp's nest
through a thousand feet

of air? Khushal says it's prayer
that keeps it clinging

to the rock face
despite the pull of gravity.

He says this place
has the power to alter lives

and on these terraces
flush with the drop

all things seem possible,
even the high path

the guide books warn against,
strewn with scree

and shifting
as the course of marriage.

Metamorphosis

First came a taste for meat
and odd bursts of irritation
like an itch along her spine.

Then she lost the urge to speak.
She'd curl up in the back room,
whole days at a time,

and at night she'd sleep-walk
through the house, nudging
at the windows and the doors,

lifting her face to the draughts,
listening to a wood louse
scratching under the apple bark.

She wondered at sofas and knives,
and no longer knew the meaning
of *milk* or the colour red,

what *hot* was and *cold*, and *nice*,
why some things shone and some
were dark, and why the baby cried.

Veneer

What the others see is the old rose
on the living room walls
and the new sage-green kitchen;
they see peacocks sipping from urns
in the ivory calm of *My Lady's Garden*.
No sign of dust or silverfish,
the tidemarks left by retreating floods
or the damage done when the lock-
out button fails on the boiler.
But when the doors are closed
and the shutters drawn, the house
has a habit of reverting.
It doesn't take long. For swarms
of ants to reappear out of the cracks
and lines of black mould to ripen
round the bath. Here already
are the pale squares that mark
where the paintings hung, the stairs
stripped of sea-grass matting,
exposing splinters and rusted nails,
that gouge where she sank a wine bottle,
substituting wood for his face.

Vanishing act

She's been shrinking
for weeks,

thinking herself
smooth and small:

curled in the back room
while he crowds the master,

she dreams of moss
and branches for walls;

and as he grows bigger
she gives ground, retreating

from the sound
in his throat, the glint

of bone against lip,
his lunge without warning.

She's paring herself
into a perfect oval,

learning to live without limbs,
refining her skin

so she's see-through,
a cluster of cells so slight

she can slip through a crack
into silence, as remote

from his rages
as a shadow on the moon.

The white room

If this were your only view
you'd be grateful for the glimmer
of crabapples. Or a cat sprawled
on a roof. Susan Trickett's
ample green bosom pressed
against the rungs of a stepladder
two doors down, anything
that anchored you still to the earth.
Every sudden flash of wings
would count. Every line
of every winter tree washed up
on the grey shore of the sky.
Take away the view and you're left
with white walls, white muslin
coiling at the windows
like some ghostly bridal gown.
Less to see. But listen
to the old stories blown in
on the wind: *Praise, my soul,*
the King of Heaven. . . The notes
come in snatches, writing
themselves on the whiteness. . .
Praise him for his . . . favour
to our fathers in distress. . .
and a wood pigeon takes you back
to the window alcove
where you sat with a book
on summer afternoons
half-listening to your mother
rattling the tea things downstairs
and that voice calling
from the evergreens: *Two cows,*
Taffy. Take two cows, Taffy. Take.

Curtains

Our son's first curtains
were sewn from the sarong
we bought on honeymoon,

dyed in shades I think of now
as devitalised,
dark wine, wet sand,

lines and swirls of colour as ragged
as the image on a foetal scan,
and the fabric so thin

when the sun shone through
those first two summers
they would flare into life,

a shadow screen
for the smallest shift of leaves
or a blackbird landing:

less like curtains then,
or sarong, than a membrane
sealing him in while he slept,

as serene as the Buddha
contemplating a circle of water
beyond his window…

We switched to blue velvet later
to block out the light
and the flesh-and-blood patterns hang

in the new house, in a room
that's sometimes spare,
sometimes his dad's, depending.

Make-believe

He piles up bedding, nightclothes,
building blocks and plastic cars
and says he's made a thunderstorm,

a pool of sharks… *Mummy,*
if they bite your legs off,
you'll have to stay for ever

and we'll be safe, like that first summer
when he'd lie curled in the corner
of his cot, as easy to miss

as the moon in daylight –

Mummy, be a witch, a nasty one,
be dinosaurus rex,
says this child like any other

who might have dropped
my hand in a dozen shopping malls
or stretched to a lifetime

those minutes we lost him in the wood;
who conjures swords from sticks,
squeezes petal-juice and calls it blood.

Stammer

He was always comfortable talking
to himself. *I've got biscuits in my bag*
and raisins and rice cakes. Vroom, vroom.
Bye, everybody. Going in Granddad's car.
Crocodiles in Mummy's bed...

He manoeuvres politely round his room,
excusing himself to a box
when he wants to reach his cupboard,
and as captain of his cushion-ship
he comments on the weather, decides

who's fallen overboard and signals
the approach of sharks. Stories
can be managed, sharks written in or out,
but there are times when his father sleeps
and sleeps, though *It's morning, Dad!*

and his mother cries into the washing-up
or talks to the wall, times
when he opens his mouth and sounds
come rattling out like conkers
from a tin, or sliding into nothing

as if he'd lost his footing
on the monkey frame...
There are times when to talk is an act
of faith, his balance suddenly so sure
I marvel, as on this March night,

stepping out into the cold and dark
in evening dress and sandals,
I hear him say without a pause
You've got to wear some socks
and Mummy your shoes are broken.

Dens

He's an expert now
at making second homes – upending
sofa cushions, draping blankets

from a table and stuffing the crevices
with football trophies
and favourite bits of rock.

He says Sunday was the best day
of his life: *Dad stayed*
for tea and no one argued.

Today is Monday
and he's huddled in the garden under a broken
tent propped up with oars,

while the crescent moon hangs
so close to Venus it could be dangling
by a thread.

After the fire

What I want to do now
is dismantle the roof
and let in the sky,

then turn the house
upside down and shake
until it all

falls out –
our disembowelled
wedding sofa,

the twisted Christening silver
and the skeleton
of the standard lamp,

our shared books fused
like the vertebrae
of some prehistoric spine.

I want to hack and scour
until every last flake
has rained

from ceilings and walls
and all that's left
is an airy whiteness

suspended in space,
like the shelters
our seven-year-old strings

amongst the green flames
of hart's tongue, stuffing in moss
for mortar, balancing

branches and sticks, lightly,
in a game of Spillikins,
across the gaps.

Evening

That bush, for instance,
a barberry with flowers so orange
they're ready to ignite,
and bees achieving lift-off,
one by one, as if tied to elastic,
and all the subtle shifts
till nightfall: how oak trees lose
their leaf amber, simplifying
to darkness in a cleft of the hills,
and that last band of cloud casts
its moorings – we can watch for these
but still not say when we saw
the first shiver of moon, or recall
the precise scent of honeysuckle.
Samuel Palmer might have painted
these cottages folding in on themselves
in the darkness, this sky careful
not to crush the hills and woods.
Swallows are roosting under that roof,
while tummocks of earth could be sheep
pulling at grass, heading for home,
and the same darkness that shelters
sleeping swallows and imagined sheep
goes on stretching and stretching, towards
its source, as if somewhere out there
we could find the edge of the frame.

What is it about moths?

Not so much the day fliers,
but the ones that come knocking
at our windowpanes in the summer dusk,
insinuating themselves
into kitchen corners or clinging
to the underside of the bathroom sill.
Soft presences lodged at the edges
of our lives. A sudden blur
of buttermilk or moss, all those creams
garlanded with brown or beige or grey
so difficult to pin down in a book.
Even their names are moody. Dark arches.
Mottled umber. Clouded border.
They're pictures just out of focus.
A reminder of otherness
and elsewhere, of only half
belonging in the world of light.

Filling the mines

No point romanticising.
They were "dismal caves"

where men picked and sawed
by candlelight – faces, tools, hands

covered in slurry –
for all the friendliness of the language,

its frigbobs and razzers,
jadding irons, scorters and whin gins.

Why would we feel safe
when every house was undermined

with shafts and roadways
stretching from Church Quarry

to Vinegar Down and Summer Lane
to the Mill,

knowing
our children's feet dangled

over a pocket of darkness
as they sat at the kitchen table

drawing monsters
and spaceships?

And why grieve now,
given their legacy

of stone-robbed
pillars and roof fall,

the crown holes where slabs of lawn
disappeared overnight,

or feel the loss
of those forests of stalactites

glittering with quartz dust,
the caverns high as a cathedral

where the old-timers used to roam
as lads, after tying a thread at the entrance

so they could trace their way
home through the dark?

Seeing God

Our seven-year-old says
his best present this Christmas
would be to see God,
but all you see from up here
is sky – and the grey-tiled roofs
across the road, each cluster
of lichen creeping along their ridges,
the solid red of a single holly,
so that what counts is not
anchorage but the wind,
and movement, starlings tumbling
in and out of the clouds,
the slow white wake of a plane,
and how at night this window
tilted to the angle of our roof
becomes a springboard and we
are divers launching
ourselves into the darkness.

Tabula rasa

At the heart of it all
were those fire sculptures,
the bowed bookshelves,

the standard lamp like the skeleton
of a long-legged bird
caught in the moment of blast,

but it was smoke that stole
into every fissure
of our lives, a storm creeping

from the horizon
of each white page,
blotting out butterflies and flowers,

smearing the walls,
sucked into cottons and silks,
nothing safe from it,

not even the wedding dress
I starved into, zippered
in its black body bag,

or that cascade
of sentimental muslin – smoke
that poured through the house

claiming books, beds, curtains, carpets, toys,
sweeping our past
like ballast out of a balloon,

until we were just so light
                                        we lifted away.

The Wellow Tumulus

"the most notable chambered long-barrow in south-western England"

Nevertheless,
it takes some finding,

keeps disappearing
from view, blotted out
by a bend in the lane or sinking
behind a fold of the hills,
hunkering down,

as if
it didn't mean to be found,
or as if the landscape
were slowly reabsorbing
its slabs of limestone
laid down in the Jurassic,
this ammonite coiled
in the door jamb
and basking in the rays
of the morning sun.

Talisman, maybe.
Or waymark.

Anyone can crawl inside
and try it for size,

as if this grave
as old as the Great Pyramid
were no more, no less
than Round Hill Tyning
or the Wellow Brook,
just a place to curl up

like a woodlouse
listening to moisture seeping
into the cells of the earth
and watch the meadow grasses dipping
against the light.

Afterwards

Cold comfort.
The thought of coming back
as horse or gadfly.
Or merging with the fabric
of forest and hill. Or even
flitting off to some hazy spirit world
equipped with flints and pottery shards
in preparation for the long haul.
I'd want this, here, now.
This muddy bridle track,
these thistles, that buzzard, those sheep.
I'd want to feel the wood of this stile
smoothed by innumerable hands,
its warmth in the sun.

Isle of the Dead

after Arnold Böcklin

The worst of it is there's nowhere
for the dead to go, no magical beyond
like the back of Lewis's wardrobe,

and death is a narrow island,
its sheer cliffs rising out of black water,
a grove of cypress trees leading

inwards, into stillness,
painting us into the dark… Unless of course
the artist got it wrong

and we're heading towards something
more akin to this hill on the edge of the city –
similar outline under a similar sky

but where clouds move,
the moon changes place and little rifts
appear in the darkness,

as in a story remembered
from childhood, that moment at dusk
when the lamplighter arrives.

Dusk

Seen from the other side
everything looks different:
the lighted lamp on the kitchen sill,
half an IKEA cushion
and the corner of an easy chair;
a son's first suit hanging
in the bedroom doorway
with its pockets waiting
to be unpicked and beyond it
the bright white banisters
and the stairs. I'm looking
through lighted windows
into someone else's life.
It looks calmer than mine,
more self-assured, and yet
the books are the same,
it's the same brand of tea
and that's my blue and white
spotted jug a stranger's
filled with cornflowers
and sweet peas. Any moment now
she's going to reach for the kettle
or glance into the garden
where I'm hovering like a moth,
half attracted to the light.

Tinnitus

Maybe it was always there.
Like that house you've walked past
on your way to work, oblivious
to its red door all these years.
A swarm of bees first registered
in a moment of stillness, buzzing
between your ears. Or what others
call ringing, whirring, whistling,
even a neighbour banging
in the upstairs flat. Or maybe
it's just the way silence sounds.
We use the same words – *sadness,*
tinnitus, red – without knowing
if we mean the same thing,
stranded, each of us, inside our heads,
as we listen to phantom sounds
and signal to one another
across a great gulf of air.

Adrift

Take this morning.
No movement but the rain falling,
no sound but the rain falling:

not a flicker of life
in the dark-eyed houses across the way,
no barking from next door.

As if life were happening
somewhere else,
this greyness simply a continuation

of last night's dreams,
the empty spaces,
missed connections.

Of course normal people
will be at work by now,
not lying in their beds

thinking the house has slipped
its moorings in the night
and drifted out to sea,

not grateful for birdsong
glistening through the rain
or that blue and white umbrella floating

past the end of the garden.

Sally's fence

I liked the old one, the low picket fence
silvered by the sun and rain that was less fence

than driftwood, less wood than air,
so broken down our two gardens almost merged

and all we saw in summer was a blur of wild roses
where the boundary should have been.

I liked the way things were before,
that free-for-all of foxgloves and columbines spilling

two-ways through the gaps,
even the badger living under Sally's shed

(she said it came from my side)
that scuffed up both our lawns.

Why choose to do what time does itself,
boxing us in, restricting the view?

I want to burn this six-foot palisade
straight as a dye that's turned our garden

into a corridor, a grave-plot,
a far cry from that childhood wilderness

where peppery phlox jostled
with acres of nettles

and all the long slow years still lay ahead.

III

Scarlet tiger

We'd have killed it
if we'd had the courage
to crush a body this
bloated or stamp on wings
like shrivelled walnuts.
Was it a mutant? Too slow
to break free and make
for the open?

It scuttled out of the leaves
and frass, climbed
our stick and hung there,
like a zippered bag crammed
with too many t-shirts,
stayed put for hours,
just shifting its footing
now and then.

We moved it on to flowers later,
offering cow parsley,
apple blossom, anything
to encourage it to feed,
then in desperation sugared water,
which left sticky pools
on the table top darkened
with wing powder.

The moth didn't budge.
For hours it clung to the same
flower head, rearranging
itself, pumping fluids
from one body part to another,

growing streamlined,
its wings slicked over its back
and as bright as if

such colours never existed
till now: this camel
and cream, the black
that in this light, at this angle,
was more a dusky green
lustred with gold –
or was it amber? – the hint
of scarlet underwing

inset like a gusset
that flashed suddenly
into prominence
as the scarlet tiger took off
from our jam jar of flowers
on the garden table, circled twice,
landed in the lilac tree,
then made its bid for the sky.

Pyramidal orchid

You've got to look close
to see what Darwin saw,
deep into the perianth, beyond

these flying skirts and outflung arms,
to grasp the precise design
of its hidden parts.

He called it perfect adaptation,
how each is configured
in relation to the rest,

lip, beak, pollinia,
and how each ridge and groove
guides the proboscis

of a butterfly or moth unerringly
to the flower's heart –
an act of providence

according to my Dad,
who was sure there was a plan
but vague about the planner

and who in a meadow such as this
would be darting
after skippers and blues

while I searched
for different types of bedstraw,
trefoil, vetch… stooping

to inspect these lilac florets
that smell not sweet but feral –
Darwin was right –

fifty or sixty semaphores
to a single spike, lifted
over the heads

of knapweed and moon daisies
and signalling furiously
through the summer air.

Valerian

As a hermit carves
his niche in the cliff face,
subsisting on berries and roots
and the small offerings
of valley dwellers, so it asks
almost nothing of the earth,
satisfied with the meanest fissure,
anchored between rocks,
but always straining
to get a little closer to the sky.

Gog and Magog

You'd almost think
they'd turned to stone,
last of a line of giants

who marched a mile westward
to the Tor, stranded now
beside a ditch,

a world away
from those flimsy willows
that witnessed the demise

of cowslips, but not
the slow rise and fall
of waters

or men's entrails smeared
around a trunk
as penalty for felling trees.

Two thousand winters
and Magog's still reaching
for the sun, sap tingling

in every twig,
despite the rot that's seeping
from her centre;

but Gog is tired
and with one last effort thrusts out
a single spray of buds

like Joseph's staff shoved
into the soil
on Wearyall Hill,

as if from this one branch might spring
a miracle too of sorts,
not a thorn tree flowering

from fashioned wood,
come Christmas,
but a whole forestful of oaks.

Parable of the Sower

after Andrew Taylor's chapel window at Great Chalfield

The wonder is
that they exist at all:
kingfisher and leaping trout,
hummingbird hawk moth
and pipistrelle bat,
the swallow and the swift,
purple loosestrife
and spiked star of Bethlehem,
this amber fox nosing
through brambles
who burns so brightly
when the sun shines through;
and the wonder is
that we make such things
as this stained glass window
where nothing chokes or withers,
nothing fails to thrive,
not the towering elm
or the partridges pecking
in the dirt, not the field poppy
or the dragonfly –
these few timely reminders
of all we stand to lose.

Kettle's Yard, Cambridge

"a continuing way of life … in which stray objects, stones, glass, pictures, sculpture are arranged in light and in space"

It's like coming home
after all these years,

to a lightness
almost forgotten,

this reverence for things
crafted or found – a huddle

of stones, for instance,
with shoulders hunched

against the wind,
or a seedhead horned

like a tribal mask –
things gracefully

co-existing, this Miró
by the door no more solid,

it seems to say,
than the browned umbel

of an allium, a painted
wildflower no lovelier

than light reflected
off a piano stool,

things separate, simple,
and connected, as the lines

of a seashell echo
the grain of scrubbed deal,

its curve the perimeter
of the table top.

Cézanne's apples, etc

Seeing those apples again,
that shimmering hillside or the shadows
of the Rue St Vincent dissolving
into splashes of lilac and blue,
the years collapse together like a fan:
love affairs, marriage, birth,
the deaths of a mother, father, friend
all occurred in the blinking
of an eye, and I'm standing here now
as then, still wanting to touch those apples
and climb that scrubby hillside
with the grasses scouring my legs,
wanting to be *there*, feeling anchored
by the forms of bushes and trees breaking up
in the heat, by imagined butterflies,
painted sunlight, painted air.

Bone china

Imagine if instead of seeping
into thirsty soil
the days of our lives

had pattern and form,
amounting to something
we could identify,

a single long poem perhaps
or a vessel we could wrap
our hands around

and hold up to the light,
a comfortable sphere
with a frieze of painted flowers brighter

than anything else in the room –
poppy, primrose,
grass-of-Parnassus –

interlaced
on a ground of flawless
glistening white.

Dimbula BOP

Not just the tea, its name
or its provenance,

these "delicate tips lightly rolled
with two carefully plucked leaves and a bud"

collected on the lush hillsides
of Ceylon,

not just the pot with a painted bee flying
over its rim

or next-door's apples yellowing on the table top,
florets of mould clustering

like barnacle-encrusted islands in sea
the colour of a tea stain,

nor the daft cat who's burrowed into a nest of twigs
intended for winter kindling

and become moss agate
set in filigree –

none of these things singly,
but their unique configuration

shining out in the darkness.

Hilltop

You see it sometimes:
the way the light strikes
a distant hill, singling out
that space between trees

like a sudden bolt
of memory, or an answer
coming through
from the other side.

Still life

after "Chinese Bowl with Cosmos" by Helen Simmonds

So this is
what it really means –

these glistening sepals,
that flush of pink at the petals' edge,

the pool of shadow
on the green-beige ground –

life stilled, all its confusion
and clamour,

as if nothing mattered for now
but five white flowers

resting their heads
on the rim of a bowl.

The studio chair

after a painting by Sara Lee Roberts

Take away the chair
and we're left with abstraction,
an empty universe stripped
of the possibility
of transcendence;

the chair reassures us:
in a downstairs room, it says,
someone is playing the piano
or laying a table, writing a note,
and it's only a matter of time

before these uprights curve
into the small of a human back;
there are noises-off –
voices from the street, perhaps,
or footsteps on the stairs –

and what we're seeing
is just a pause in the action,
an abandoned prop
from the world of Post-It notes
and piano lessons, stranded

in a pool of light
from an unseen window,
as if the stillness concealed
some invisible presence
and sunshine itself were the sitter.

Eve speaks

after Henri Rousseau's "The Dream"

This is his dream, mind.
This hothouse gloom,
the fleshy lotus flowers,
his darling shock-eyed lions
blundering through the bushes.
Would I have chosen
to lounge naked on one hip
purely for his delectation,
with his foliage reaching out
to finger me? To affect
this studio pose, drawing-room
smile, while pretending
to be so pleased with life?
Frozen for eternity
in someone else's dream.
Adam's. Henri's. Even God's.
Take your pick. (You'll see
that none of them are here.)
Let the charmer fumble
his notes. I'm all ears. Ready
for a bite of that forbidden fruit,
dozens of whose golden orbs
are dangling overhead.
Just let me out of Eden.
Give me a windy headland,
the vanilla scent of gorse
and adders basking
among the bracken,
some earnest little ship
beating her way southwards
through the waves, just a smudge
on the far horizon.

Those were the days...

for Elizabeth Crisp (1954-2009)

What would you have said, Lizzie: were they the days,
my friend? Hearing the old songs played

at your funeral, I think of bodies crammed
in small dark college rooms

drinking cheap red wine and breathing air
so laced with dope just being there

made us high, of rushing to lose
ourselves, anxious to keep up, to know who

was sleeping with who, of acid trips and speed
and how in honour of Lou Reed

you got us dancing on the wild side,
wildest of our little sisterhood.

Always one step ahead, even at the end
you were still joking, promising to send

a message in a bottle giving us all the answers. Were those
the days, dear Lizzie, lived largely in a haze

of altered states? Was the song
both right and wrong?

Either way, you'd have settled for dull
given half a chance. For our slow casseroles,

our tidy garden borders. And sitting on a bench
with Milou in the sun.

Leopard country

Their lives recede
in a blur of water, leaf and sky,
barely anchored by a date,
a couple of words in spidery writing:
"leopard country, 5th July 1936";
"Nagalapuram Hills,
where we saw the panther".
There's little for the eye
to rest on: a wooden roof glinting
beneath cloud-covered slopes,
dhoongas on the Jamuna
en route for Kashmir.
And tiny distant people,
like those two fishermen
crouching in a line of surf,
bodies black against the foam,
or our mother sitting
with her knees drawn up
on a picnic rug, next
to my father's jungle hat,
a flask, two fat white mugs
and what surely
must be a sugar bowl.

Love that Pink

Enter my mother

not in the latter-day sheepskin
or that sad brown scarf

but sweeping across our lawns
in a cream dress splashed

with enormous flowers,
wearing lipstick

with a name like Confidential,
Coralissima, Love that Pink,

or dangling her legs
over the Madmati

and squinting into the sun
under a cocked hat,

game for anything.

Samsara

He is more than himself,
a boy just out of his bath,
wrapped in a towel and reading
under the light, so still
he could be a golden Buddha
in some temple eyrie,
not so much a body illuminated
as the source of all stillness
and light – except that this
is my son, his skin shining,
his blond head bent over
his book, sitting so close
I could almost touch him,
so far away I'm gazing at him
across the roof of the world.

Slideshow

Tintagel, 8 July 2006

Click on the arrows
and it happens again – a flash
of sky, light juddering
on the sea, the sudden appearance
of a plimsolled foot.
Not stills of Tintagel, these,
but pure accidents.
Miniature sequences
of homemade video – the time
it takes for a plume of spray
to fly up and then freeze,
a ribbon of water to slide
over the sand. Click on the arrows
and there's that dog running
six paces through the waves,
a seagull folding its wings;
there's our son staring
into the light that's flooding
through Merlin's Cave,
while the wind snatches up
a strand of his hair,
over and over.

Salt marshes

All that's left of the spinney
are two dead trees, some scattered driftwood
silvered by the salt winds,

and for the bladder campion too,
the stonecrop and sea thrift
it's only a matter of time,

for the salt bushes in whose wiry arms
tiny spectral crabs were abandoned
by the last storm tide.

Nothing defends
these margins between
the meadows and the sea

where we're walking, already past
the mid-point of our lives,
struggling, she and I,

to catch up with our sons
as they head for the car and their PSPs –
out of earshot now,

two small bright figures striding
into the distance
without a backward glance.

Flight WY02

I can follow your flight
all the way to Muscat
and on to Kathmandu,
comforted by a miniature plane
and a pink arrow pointing
across my computer screen,
track your position
as you speed through the sky
over Holland and hours
out of sync – night time here,
morning there – begin your descent
towards Oman. Too late
I remember the mints,
stuff I meant to say,
like *Ask them for a blanket*
if you're cold. Then out of the blue
you're back in the playground
releasing your balloon
along with the rest, tilting
your head to watch it go,
willing it on, the sky
full of them and a prize
for the one that flies furthest.

Waiting for the Perseid meteors

Not the promised rain of stars
but shifting archipelagos
with dark straits flowing in between,

then darkness
stripped of cloud and packed
with so many points of light they merge

like luminous grains of sand;
not that sky-full of arrows they're seeing
in Ramona or on Smetovi Mountain,

but a single burst of brilliance
as ice and dust, swept
through billions of years,

burns up at last in Earth's atmosphere
and is witnessed from this speck
in space and time – a suburban garden

where a cat is rummaging in the undergrowth
and crickets scrape their wings
together to attract a mate.

Wishing tree

The tree itself is a miracle,
ten miles of twigs and branches,
a hundred thousand leaves,
and look how we've wound
our streamers of paper and cloth
in the apple-green glow,
around this waterfall of roots,
longing to connect, longing
for answers from somewhere
beyond ourselves – never
quite at home in the moment,
the moment never enough,
even now as clouds mirror
the contours of summer,
as the breeze shivers
that clump of harebells
and the chalk path winds
its way over the brow
of the hill like a ribbon
of water, a ribbon of light.